*S*poil the *V*ines

Little Foxes That Spoil the Vines

W. Barry Miller

HERALD PRESS

Waterloo, Ontario

Scottdale, Pennsylvania

Canadian Cataloguing in Publication Data
Miller, W. Barry, 1944-
     Little foxes that spoil the vines
Includes bibliographical references.
ISBN 0-8361-9056-4
1. Sin, Venial. I. Title.
BV4625.6.M54 1996 241'.3 C96-931756-5

LITTLE FOXES THAT SPOIL THE VINES
Copyright © 1997 by Herald Press, Waterloo, Ont. N2L 6H7
    Published simultaneously in USA by Herald Press,
    Scottdale, Pa. 15683. All rights reserved
Library of Congress Catalog Card Number: 96-78091
Canadiana Entry Number: C96-931756-5
International Standard Book Number: 0-8361-9056-4
Printed in the United States of America
Cover and inside art by Valerie Briggs
Book and cover design by Paula M. Johnson

06 05 04 03 02 01 00 99 98 97 10 9 8 7 6 5 4 3 2 1

To my best friend,
My life partner, my lover,
My soul mate,
My wife, Loris

Contents

Foreword

Small irritations and problems can eat away at the beauty and love relationship of life," says author, W. Barry Miller.

In *Little Foxes That Spoil the Vines,* Miller points out the danger of ignoring "little sins" and allowing them to grow.

These peccadilloes are skillfully portrayed metaphorically in six foxes, from the gray fox of hurtful words to the black fox of doubt. Such little foxes can ruin our vineyards and destroy our lives if left to run wild.

Miller offers practical suggestions for capturing and controlling these foxes before damage is done.

I commend this book for the strengthening of our life with God, with self, and with others. This wisdom will help us hunt down those pesky foxes and be set free to keep bearing fruit for God.

—*Susan Titus Osborn*
Editor, The Christian Communicator
Fullerton, California

Foreword

Little Foxes That Spoil the Vines could be called a book for spiritual renewal. It probes deeply into our attitudes and the subtle sins of the spirit, which spoil life's meaning, effectiveness, and relationships with God and others.

Here is an insightful look at these inner temptations which so easily overtake the strong as well as the weak—especially the strong. "If you think you are standing, watch out that you do not fall" (1 Cor. 10:12).

However, there is more. The chapters are biblical and Christ-centered. For each sidetracking allurement, there is a solution. Miller shows the way toward deliverance and healing from these harmful attitudes and sins of the spirit.

With such counsel, the author encourages us to "grow up in every way ... into Christ," "to maturity, to the measure of the full stature of Christ" (Eph. 4:13-15). My prayer is that you will be spiritually renewed as you ponder these insights.

—John M. Drescher
Harrisonburg, Virginia

Preface

IN 1853 George Burrowes wrote a commentary on the Song of Solomon. This volume was reprinted more than a century later by the Banner of Truth.

In his foreword written from Westminster Chapel in London, Dr. D. M. Lloyd-Jones states that Burrowes' commentary has the characteristics of learning and scholarship, accuracy and carefulness, but above all and more important than all else, true spiritual insight and understanding. It provides a key to the understanding of the whole and of every verse, which the humblest Christian can easily follow.

A key verse in the Song of Solomon (2:15, KJV) provides the title and launching pad for this book.

> Take us the foxes,
> the little foxes, that spoil the vines;
> for our vines have tender grapes.

Commenting on this verse, Burrowes informs us that foxes, jackals, and little foxes are quite common in Palestine. They are especially fond of grapes. The foxes often burrow holes in hedges around the gardens and uproot vines. Unless strictly watched, they would destroy whole vineyards. People sometimes ate the flesh of foxes in the autumn, when they were grown fat from feeding on grapes.

Aesop (ca. 550 B.C.) knows that a fox likes grapes; one of his fables has a fox calling grapes sour if they are out of reach. Aristophanes, the Athenian dramatist (died ca. 388 B.C.), compares soldiers to foxes, because both consume the grapes of the countries through which they pass. We hear a gripe about grapes and foxes from a Greek poet, Theocritus (died ca. 250 B.C.):

> I hate the foxes with their bushy tails,
> Which numerous spoil the grapes of Micon's vines
> When fall the evening shades.

Jesus mentions the holes dug by foxes (Luke 9:58). Shakespeare knows about destructive grasping for grapes:

> Who buys a minute's mirth to wail a week?
> Or sells eternity to get a toy?
> For one sweet grape who will the vine destroy?
>
> — *"The Rape of Lucrece"*

In the Song of Solomon, the foxes represent anything which injures, by stealth and cunning, the graces of those who are the objects of divine love. Accordingly, Jesus calls Herod Antipas a fox, since he is an enemy of God's people (Luke 13:32).

Burrowes explains how Solomon teaches that those who are favored richly with grace, those whom our Lord is drawing toward heaven, will be careful to guard against sin, especially little sins.

Earlier in the Song of Solomon, we read the lament, "My own vineyard I have not kept" (1:6). Now this verse about the little foxes (2:15) calls us to guard the vineyard of the heart against the inroads of anything, however trifling, that may corrode and destroy our graces.

Too often we may have been like a boy depicted by Theocritus, who was sent to watch a vineyard. He became so absorbed in weaving a chaplet of flowers that he did not notice two foxes among the vines. One was stealthily plundering food, while the other was making havoc with the grapevines.

When we are most deeply filled with the love of Jesus, then we are most careful in watching out for sin. We zealously guard ourselves against the slightest sins.

The services of the Jewish tabernacle taught the necessity of holiness, even in trivial things. Through little sins, Satan begins the most deadly temptations. He attacks us in unexpected quarters, in unlooked-for ways. The time for resisting him is at the beginning of his insidious assaults.

When we indulge in what seem to be trifling departures from watchfulness and duty, we may not count the costs. But these sallies into sin will blind our minds to the truth of Scripture, corrode and enfeeble our graces, and grieve the Holy Spirit.[1]

We need to catch these little foxes that ruin our vineyards. Let us direct our thought life toward what is honorable and our actions toward what we know is right (Phil. 4:8-9). Then the God of peace will be with us as we watch ourselves in all diligence, praying without ceasing:

> Search me, O God, and know my heart;
> try me and know my thoughts;
> And see if there be any wicked way in me,
> and lead me in the way everlasting.
>
> *—Psalm 139:23, KJV*

Acknowledgments

I acknowledge the contribution of the late Dr. Jerry Hayner, pastor and personal friend, whose sermons and life provided the inspiration and conceptual framework for this book. He often talked about the abundant life in Christ (John 10:10b).

It is my sincere prayer that this book will provide encouragement and support to those readers who seek to rid their lives of the little foxes that ruin the vines and experience life more abundantly.

I am grateful for the professional word-processing services of Heather Cull of Software Excellence. Her encouragement and enthusiasm for this work is most appreciated.

I am honored to have the beautiful artwork of Valerie Briggs of the United Kingdom to adorn this book. Valerie is president of the Worchester Society of Artists and is recognized as a distinguished wildlife artist.

I also thank my son Chad and my son Justin and daughter-in-law, Karen, for their continual encouragement and support.

To God alone be the glory!

—*W. Barry Miller*

CHAPTER ONE

Fox Hunting with the King

On their return the apostles told Jesus all they had done. He took them with him and withdrew privately to a city called Bethsaida. When the crowds found out about it, they followed him; and he welcomed them, and spoke to them about the kingdom of God, and healed those who needed to be cured.

The day was drawing to a close, and the twelve came to him and said, "Send the crowd away, so that they may go into the surrounding villages and countryside to lodge and get provisions; for we are here in a deserted place." But he said to them, "You give them something to eat." They said, "We have no more than five loaves and two fish—unless we are to go and buy food for all these people." For there were about five thousand men. And he said to his disciples, "Make them sit down in groups of about fifty each." They did so and made them all sit down. And taking the five loaves and the two fish, he looked up to heaven, and blessed and broke them, and gave them to the disciples to set before the crowd. And all ate and were filled. What was left over was gathered up, twelve baskets of broken pieces. (Luke 9:10-17)

> Take us the foxes,
> the little foxes, that spoil the vines;
> for our vines have tender grapes.
> — *Song of Solomon 2:15*

> Throw me a kiss from across the room,
> Say I look nice when I'm not,
> A line a day when you're far away,
> Little things mean a lot.

B ack during the so-called happy days, the 1950s, over the airwaves came the lyrics of that song, "Little Things Mean a Lot."

Most of us are size-conscious people. We have been made that way by many tangible and intangible things and by influences in our times. The emphasis on physical fitness has made each of us aware of our own size. The emphasis on privacy has impressed us with the size of our houses. The emphasis on energy consumption has opened our eyes to the size of our automobiles. On and on we could go.

A spaceship to the moon now makes a jet traveling faster than the speed of sound seem obsolete. A jumbo 747 that can carry five hundred people makes a Boeing 707 seem inferior. Our newspapers constantly remind us of big cities, big business, big money. The little man, the little needs, the little considerations have been sucked into the intake valves of our fast-moving society. Our values have been perverted.

Perhaps that is why the masses who live below the subsistence level are clamoring to be heard from valleys of squalor. "When we burn down your cities, when we loot your stores, then maybe you'll notice us," they say.

In many homes, the little people called children are not listened to, noticed, or considered until the phone rings after midnight and the voice on the other end of the line says, "We have your son down at the police station. Can you come as quickly as possible?" Perhaps the daughter defiantly announces to her parents, "Well, I'm pregnant. Now maybe you'll listen."

In the Scriptures we are told, "In the beginning God created the sun and the moon; he made the stars also" (Gen. 1). It is stated almost as if the stars were an afterthought. Yet who is to deny the importance of the stars? In the midwestern United States, cyclones sweep through the plains and take in their wake crops worth thousands of dollars. Yet annually more damage is done by grasshoppers than by cyclones.

Little things mean a lot. Maybe that's why Solomon, the wise king, says, "Catch us the foxes, the little foxes, that ruin the vineyards—for our vineyards are in blossom" (NRSV). We cannot measure it, but I am confident that more people are lost to the kingdom of God by the so-called little things that Christians do than by the big sins we commit. I am also sure that we are deprived of a great deal of peace in our lives, not by big events that disappoint us, but by the little things that sap our energy and ruin our spirits.

"Catch us the foxes, the little foxes, that spoil the vineyards—for our vineyards are in blossom."

Those words of Solomon were originally spoken in the love sonnet he wrote. They were included in the context where the bride was speaking her endearing words to her husband. Palestine was infested with little foxes. They damaged the vineyards by eating many new blossoms and thus cutting back the growth of the grapes. The beauty and productiveness of a vineyard would be reduced by the invasion of these pests. In like manner, small irritations and problems can eat away at the beauty and love relationships of life.

Tennyson says,

> It is the little rift within the lute,
> That by and by will make the music mute,
> And ever widening slowly silence all.[2]

Therefore, with the blast of the bugle, the neighing of the horses, and the barking of frisky dogs, let us go with the King in search of the little foxes that come to dig into our lives and sap the vines of our productivity. As we begin the hunt, let us guard against several common mistakes.

Our first mistake is to ignore little things. We treat them as if they don't matter when they really do. I am not proposing that we should be so picky as to confront every little grievance. Not at all! I am suggesting that the little irritating things of life can prevent us from enjoying the bigger events. Try walking through a beautiful rose garden with a tiny piece of gravel in your shoe. You'll be amazed at how you miss the roses. Try looking at a gorgeous sunset with a tiny speck lodged in your eye.

Our second mistake is to forget that little things have the capacity to grow. If the grievance doesn't grow in my mind, sometimes it grows in the mind of the other person and becomes a real stumbling block in our relationship.

Some time ago, a lion cub won its place in the hearts of millions of moviegoers. In *Born Free,* this frisky little animal rolled and tumbled, jumped and sped on its way over hill after hill. Later, it had to be put to death. It had grown up and had turned on its owner.

Sometimes little things do get larger, and if they are not properly dealt with, they can do great damage.

So catch us the foxes, the little foxes, that spoil the vines by telling us not to worry about the little sins we commit, as though only the big sins count.

In the Sermon on the Mount, King Jesus searched for the little foxes (Matt. 5–7). The people he addressed were concerned about the big foxes. They were uptight about murder. They wanted all murderers to be put to death. But the King was concerned about anger and hatred. Without these, there would be no murder. He fought against the little foxes.

The people were upset about those who broke up homes

by committing adultery. But the King was upset about the way people view the opposite sex as objects solely for one's own satisfaction, as things and not people, as toys and not persons. He was bothered about the look of lust, about selfishly desiring another's body for personal pleasure and no more.

Get rid of the little fox, and you will have no problem with it growing larger. Take care of the thoughts, and you don't have to worry about the acts.

The people were angry at robbers who slipped into their homes under the cloak of darkness and took their possessions. But the King was bothered about the frame of mind that leads to a person coveting, desiring another's possessions, thinking that the good life *does* consist in the abundance of things (Luke 12:15).

Most of us are not nearly as bothered as we ought to be about the little foxes—jealousies, bitter spirits, excessive worry, anxiety, pride. . . . We can think of a million bigger things that deserve our attention. So we go on assuaging our consciences.

Catch us the foxes, the little foxes, that ruin our vineyards, the little sins that deprive us of peace of mind, the things we do like complaining, criticizing, gossiping, and so on. Such things limit our witness for Christ.

The writer of Hebrews says, "Let us also lay aside every weight and the sin that clings so closely, and let us run with perseverance the race that is set before us" (12:1).

Catch us the foxes, the little foxes telling us that we are not important, that our deeds do not matter because they are so small and insignificant in comparison to others.

How the citizens of Jericho laughed when they saw Joshua's army of itinerant soldiers marching around their city walls, holding rams' horns in their hands! How the Philistines must have laughed when they saw Samson with a jawbone of an ass in his hand, getting ready to fight a whole battalion of soldiers! Remember the obvious amusement of Goliath when he faced David, the shepherd boy, who was armed only with a sling and a few small stones.

Jesus' law of greatness magnifies little things. "Whoever wishes to become great among you must be your servant, and whoever wishes to be first among you must be slave of all" (Mark 10:43-44).

A boy's lunch was all that the disciples could find, but it became a feast for five thousand people (John 6:9; Luke 9:12-17). Two small copper coins were all a widow had to offer in the house of the Lord, but those coins became the largest gift anyone ever gave. Jesus honored it (Luke 21:1-4).

On the campus of Oxford University in London, three young men began to burn for Christ. Their souls and spirits were ablaze with the glory of God which was consuming them. The result was the Methodist movement.

At the conclusion of the Civil War, the Southern Baptist Seminary, Greenville, South Carolina, was in deep trouble. Its future was in jeopardy. Then a group of the professors along with the president met and said, "Let us solemnly agree to let the seminary die. But let us die first."

God used their efforts to keep a dream alive. Since that time, thousands of men and women have come forth from those hallowed halls as heralds of Christ.

God never counts people—he measures them. The Lord began by calling "uneducated and ordinary" people as those upon whom to build the church. Through the ages, he has multiplied their efforts a thousand times (Acts 4:13).

What you do is important in the eyes of God. It is important because you are important, made in God's image. What you do has value because you have value. There are no little people in the kingdom of God. We are all big!

Catch us the foxes, the little foxes telling us that the seeds we sow will not bear much fruit.

Isaiah says,

> For as the rain and the snow come down from heaven,
> and do not return there, until they have watered the earth,
> making it bring forth and sprout,
> giving seed to the sower and bread to the eater,
> So shall my word be that goes out from my mouth;
> it shall not return to me empty,
> but it shall accomplish that which I purpose,
> and succeed in the thing for which I sent it.
>
> *—Isaiah 55:10-11*

Albert Elliott prayed,

> Help me forget, dear Lord
> The things which hurt me so!—
> The thoughtless, unkind word—
> Discouragements I know.

Let not despondency,
Whate'er the cause may be,
Destroy my confidence
In others—and in Thee.

Give me the strength I need
To overcome the fear—
Thy hand of Love to lead,
A heart to persevere.

Out of the shadows then,
And into the heavenly light,
And peace restored again,
I'll rise to nobler height.[3]

Don't ever underestimate the power of the seed!

Three little girls and their father were left alone after the death of the mother. The father had always left the so-called religious matters up to his wife. The oldest daughter tried to take her mother's place. She cooked, bathed the children, and put them to bed at night. Always before she turned out the light, she offered a prayer. One night, the youngest child wanted to pray. She said, "Dear God, you have taken my mommy away, and now I have no mommy to pray for me. Please help me."

The father happened to hear those words. It was a planted seed. In the quietness of his bedroom that night, the seed was watered with the tears of his repentance. Before morning came, the seed had brought forth its fruit in his conversion.

I am only one, but I am one—one for whom Christ died, one in whom Christ can live and work, one who is responsible for every little thing I do.

CHAPTER TWO

In Search of the Gray Fox

Not many of you should become teachers, my brothers and sisters, for you know that we who teach will be judged with greater strictness. For all of us make many mistakes. Anyone who makes no mistakes in speaking is perfect, able to keep the whole body in check with a bridle. If we put bits into the mouths of horses to make them obey us, we guide their whole bodies. Or look at ships: though they are so large that it takes strong winds to drive them, yet they are guided by a very small rudder wherever the will of the pilot directs. So also the tongue is a small member, yet it boasts of great exploits.

How great a forest is set ablaze by a small fire! And the tongue is a fire. The tongue is placed among our members as a world of iniquity; it stains the whole body, sets on fire the cycle of nature, and is itself set on fire by hell. For every species of beast and bird, of reptile and sea creature, can be tamed and has been tamed by the human species, but no one can tame the tongue—a restless evil, full of deadly poison. With it we bless the Lord and Father, and with it we curse those who are made in the likeness of God. From the same mouth come blessing and cursing. My brothers and sisters, this ought not to be so. Does a spring pour forth from the same opening both fresh and brackish water? Can a fig tree, my brothers and sisters, yield olives, or a grapevine figs? No more can salt water yield fresh.

Who is wise and understanding among you? Show by your good life that your works are done with gentleness born of wisdom. (James 3:1-13)

> Take us the foxes,
> the little foxes, that spoil the vines;
> for our vines have tender grapes.

How big is big? How small is small? Size is relative. What might not seem to be much to one person can be gigantic to another. A dollar might be easily expendable for a person who has a thousand of them, but for a beggar on the street, it might buy enough nourishment for a day.

The fox is little, so it seems, but since it can destroy the blossoms which would eventually produce the grapes, suddenly it is not small anymore.

So "catch us the foxes, the little foxes, that ruin the vineyards—for our vineyards are in blossom." This time, let us search for the little gray foxes.

Gray is a color neither black nor white, yet it combines qualities of both. When we speak of a questionable deal, we call it "shady." There is a gray quality about it. A joke or story that is indiscreet is often called "off-color," gray. There are other areas of our lives that come across as gray to those who associate with us.

Some deeds are not white, not pure in quality. They may not be all black, all bad, or completely empty of value, just gray. Grayness in life can often be devastating. Better black or white, for at least then we know where we stand. Better cold or hot (Rev. 3:15-16). But gray? Well, we are not sure.

Perhaps nowhere is this grayness more evident than in our use of words or in our lack of words. We reveal more about ourselves with words than we suspect. Words are vehicles which carry our thoughts from our brain to the brain of another person. They express our ideas, our feelings, our sentiments.

Some say, "Sticks and stones may break my bones, but words will never hurt me." Don't believe it! Words spoken in anger have done irreparable damage to feelings.

Profane words, curse words, unkind words, critical words, lying words—all leave sticky smudges on the painted walls of our lives.

A lot of relationships exist in a state of grayness because of the use of words. Some people do not communicate their love with their words; instead, they communicate toleration or even dislike. Yet, maybe deep down, love really does exist. Others do not use words at all to communicate their feelings. Life is gray when a person never hears the words "I love you," "I need you," "I appreciate you."

In his youth, Brooke Adams, son of one-time United States ambassador to Great Britain, Charles Francis Adams, made this entry in his diary:

> Went fishing with my father . . .
> the most glorious day of my life.

So great was the influence of that personal experience with his father that for thirty years thereafter, he made repeated references in his diary to the glowing memory of that one day.

The rest of the story is sad. When Charles Francis Adams died, his son, then an adult, searched through his father's diary and found that day. The entry read:

> Went fishing with my son . . .
> a day wasted.

Words! It matters how we use them. It matters what we say.

It is one thing to tell your wife or sweetheart that she is a "vision," and it is quite another to tell her she is a "sight." She will be complimented if you tell her that when you look at her, "time stands still." But do not tell her that her face would "stop a clock." You may call her a "chick," but be careful if you call her a "hen."

James says,

> Likewise the tongue is a small part of the body, but it makes great boasts. Consider what a great forest is set on fire by a

small spark. The tongue also is a fire, a world of evil among the parts of the body. It corrupts the whole person, sets the whole course of his life on fire, and is itself set on fire by hell.

—James 3:5-6

Where shall I look for this fox, this little gray fox that destroys the tender blossoms of life? I'll listen to the words, the little words, the descriptive words—all the words people use to express themselves.

One man has said, "I'd rather be swallowed by a whale than be nibbled to death by minnows." Words can be the minnows, silver-gray minnows that nibble away the vitality of life.

Listen to the profane words that people use. They are a mark of manhood, of maturity, we say. They indicate sophistication and freedom. We show our mental toughness when we use profanity.

However, words become so much a part of us that once we begin using them, we have difficulty in losing them. Speech patterns are formed and each person has a basic vocabulary. We use those same words over and over. We have difficulty in refraining from using profane words if they become much a part of our lives.

The Christian must make discriminate use of words. Like the non-Christian, the believer feels strongly about disappointments. In stressful times, a swear word might seem to be the best way to express anger and disgust.

We make rash promises and call upon God, a god, or a

substitute, trying to manipulate that higher power to witness to the truth of what we say or intend to do. Thus Jezebel told the prophet Elijah, "So may the gods do to me, and more also, if I do not make your life like the life of one of [the slain prophets of Baal] by this time tomorrow" (1 Kings 19:2).

However, James says,

> Above all, my beloved, do not swear, either by heaven or by earth or by any other oath, but let your "Yes" be yes and your "No" be no, so that you may not fall under condemnation.
> —James 5:11-12

James is faithfully teaching what Jesus commands:

> Do not swear at all,
> either by heaven, for it is the throne of God,
> or by the earth, for it is his footstool,
> or by Jerusalem, for it is the city of the great King.
> Let your word be "Yes, Yes" or "No, No";
> anything more than this comes from the evil one.
> —Matthew 5:34-36

I am convinced that the witness of many Christians has been severely damaged and handicapped by their inability to control their tongues when they are angry. Catch us the foxes, the little gray foxes that destroy the vines, for our vines have tender blossoms.

Where shall I look for this fox? I'll listen to the words, the little words of untruth which we use to gain what we desire. People all around us tell lies. The youngest children and sometimes the oldest adults lie. People use lies to gain their desires or to cover guilt.

Lying comes in many shapes and sizes. In government, we call it the "credibility gap," in big business it is "expediency," and in human relations, it is the "white lie."

How is it done? Sometimes it is total prevarication, an absolute untruth. Other times, it is a mixture of truth and error. Still other times, it is by implication or inference; in that case the liar who is caught can claim, "I didn't say that," "I didn't mean it that way," or "They must have misunderstood me."

The writer of Proverbs says,

> Lying lips are an abomination to the Lord.
> —*Proverbs 12:22*
> What is desirable in a person is loyalty,
> and it is better to be poor than a liar.
> —*Proverbs 19:22*

When Christians allow their words to become gray in regard to truth, then their words about Christ are questioned by unbelievers. Catch us the foxes, the little gray foxes, that lie and cannot be trusted.

Where shall I find the little gray fox? I shall ponder a person's words about another person.

Gossip is a disease. It is sinful and destructive right along with selfishness, greed, and lust. Gossip is a fox that must be captured. It may eat more tender blossoms than all of the other gray foxes.

The gossiper through the use of words, with intent or

sometimes carelessly and without intent, hurts and even destroys the character of another person.

Wise people say that our reports about other people should pass three tests:

> Is it true?
> Is it kind?
> Is it necessary?

I heard about someone who, when asked to listen to gossip about another person, would take from his pocket a notepad and write down what he heard. Then he would ask for the storyteller's signature after the notes so he could validate the words he had heard. People learned to respect his integrity.

Maybe it would be a good idea if you and I would not tell anything to which we would be unwilling to sign our names.

Who is this gray fox? He is a person who enjoys the limelight. When he snares unfortunate news about another person, he is standing center stage. Sometimes he himself is a guilty person. When he is relating the failures and sins of another, somehow he is giving some relief to himself for his own guilt. He or she can be a vicious person. With their tongues, gossipers assassinate victims, destroy their character, and kill their spirits.

Yet this is a sly fox. It can eat at our vines before we are aware of its presence. An old proverb says,

> Beware, for the dog that fetches a bone will carry a bone.

The one who tells a tale to you today might tell

one about you tomorrow.

Catch us the foxes, the little gray foxes of gossip, and put them to death because they are destroying the tender blossoms. I am convinced that there would be fewer gray foxes if people were more concerned about healing than hurting, about saving a life than destroying a life.

Where shall I find the gray fox? I'll listen to the words that people use with each other.

A game we have learned from popular television shows is the put-down. This can be a safe game or a sorry one. I have a feeling that most people are already experiencing enough pain and rejection in life without experiencing any more.

"What do you have in common?" a psychiatrist asked one couple. The woman answered, "One thing. Neither of us can stand the other."

When John Milton's wife was referred to as a rose, the unhappily married poet remarked, "I am no judge of flowers, but it may be so, for I feel the thorns daily."

Life gets tense, nerves become frayed, tempers flare—but God's Word still says,

> Be kind to one another, tenderhearted,
> forgiving one another
> as God in Christ has forgiven you.
> —*Ephesians 4:32*

A preacher tells the story of a couple several years ago: the wife was a Christian, and the husband was not. The preacher thought the dear lady was a kindhearted and tender person. While talking with her husband about his relationship with God, the preacher mentioned the wife's faith and practice. The husband said, "Preacher, my wife is a chronic complainer. She constantly nags about everything. She lies, she gossips, and she can turn her Christianity on and off like a water fountain. If that's what being a Christian is all about, I want no part of it."

A few months later the preacher was called to preach at the husband's funeral. The preacher wondered if the husband had ever accepted Christ. If he had not, was his wife the fox that destroyed the tender blossoms where faith might have grown?

The only way to be rid of that fox, that gray fox, is to surrender our lives to the lordship of Jesus Christ. Our words are not going to be any better than our spirits, and Christ can change us from the inside out.

Paul says,

> If I speak in the tongues of mortals and of angels,
> but do not have love,
> I am a noisy gong or a clanging cymbal.
> And if I have prophetic powers,
> and understand all mysteries and all knowledge,
> and if I have all faith, so as to remove mountains,
> but do not have love,
> I am nothing.
>
> —*1 Corinthians 13:1-3*

Love can kill the fox. It is time we started hunting!

FOR REFLECTION

The Gray Fox of Hurtful Words

On a windswept hill in an English country churchyard stands a drab, gray slate tombstone. Bleak and unpretentious, it leans slightly to one side, beaten slick and thin by blasts of weather. The quaint stone bears an epitaph not easily seen unless one stoops over and looks closely. The faint etchings read,

> Beneath this stone, a lump of clay,
> lies Arabella Young,
> Who, on the twenty-forth of May
> began to hold her tongue.[4]

Without a tongue, no mother could sing her baby to sleep tonight. Without use of language, no ambassador could adequately represent our nation. No teacher could stretch the minds of students. No attorney could defend the truth in court. No pastor could comfort troubled souls. No complicated, controversial issue could be discussed and solved.

Without language and communication media, our entire world would be reduced to unintelligible grunts and shrugs. Seldom do we pause to consider just how valuable our tongues are.

However, the tongue is as volatile as it is vital.

> The tongue is a fire, . . .
> a restless evil,
> full of deadly poison.
>
> —*James 3:6, 8*

Many people have offered counsel on how to keep our tongues checked and caged. William Norris, the American journalist, specialized in simple rhymes. He wrote:

> If your lips would keep from slips,
> Five things observe with care:
> To whom you speak; of whom you speak;
> And how, and when, and where.[5]

King David put it more bluntly in Psalm 39:1.

> I will guard my ways
> that I may not sin with my tongue:
> I will keep a muzzle on my mouth.

An anonymous poet expressed these sentiments:

> May I softly walk and wisely speak,
> Lest I harm the strong or wound the weak;
> For all those wounds I yet must feel,
> And bathe in love until they heal.
> Why should I carelessly offend,
> Since many of life's joys depend
> On gentle words and peaceful ways;
> Which spread such brightness o'er our days.[6]

Ruth Harms Calkin offered this prayer:

> O dear God
> Words can be so devastating,
> So destructive.
> They shock and numb.
> They sting and torment.
> In three brief minutes,

They can disfigure a soul.
They permeate the air
Like a suffocating poison.
Lord, Your own Word convicts us:
"So also the tongue is a small thing,
But what enormous damage it can do."
Teach us to cope tactfully
Even in moments of disagreement.
Make us carefully selective
And lovingly protective
In the creative use of words.[7]

ENCOURAGEMENT FROM SCRIPTURE

Rash words are like sword thrusts,
but the tongue of the wise brings healing.
—Proverbs 12:18

To watch over mouth and tongue is to keep out of trouble.
—Proverbs 21:23

Let no evil talk come out of your mouths,
but only what is useful for building up as there is need,
so that your words may give grace to those who hear.
—Ephesians 4:29

A soft answer turns away wrath,
but a harsh word stirs up anger.
The tongue of the wise dispenses knowledge,
but the mouths of fools pour out folly.
—Proverbs 15:1-2

A gentle tongue is a tree of life,
but perverseness in it breaks the spirit.

—Proverbs 15:4

Those who desire life and desire to see good days,
let them keep their tongues from evil
and their lips from speaking deceit.

—1 Peter 3:10

CHAPTER THREE

In Search of the Red Fox

Now this I affirm and insist on in the Lord: you must no longer live as the Gentiles live, in the futility of their minds. They are darkened in their understanding, alienated from the life of God because of their ignorance and hardness of heart. They have lost all sensitivity and have abandoned themselves to licentiousness, greedy to practice every kind of impurity. That is not the way you learned Christ! For surely you have heard about him and were taught in him, as truth is in Jesus. You were taught to put away your former way of life, your old self, corrupt and deluded by its lusts, and to be renewed in the spirit of your minds, and to clothe yourselves with the new self, created according to the likeness of God in true righteousness and holiness.

So then, putting away falsehood, let all of us speak the truth to our neighbors, for we are members of one another. Be angry but do not sin; do not let the sun go down on your anger, and do not make room for the devil. *(Eph. 4:17-27)*

Take us the foxes,
the little foxes, that spoil the vines;
for our vines have tender grapes.

L earning to live with our past is one of the greatest chal-
lenges we shall ever have in life. The human mind is
like a massive storage vault. It absorbs every detail of
every experience we have. Indeed, every moment the eyes are
open, they are photographing what they see and developing
these pictures in the darkroom of the mind.

The mind is a phenomenal collector of facts and data, and
it does not yield them up to just any key. Hence, we have a
blessing, but we also might have a curse.

Most people have been wronged by others, either inten-
tionally, or unintentionally, directly or indirectly. Most people do
not receive the appreciation they are due. Others do not recog-
nize that the person's real self is worth more than all worldly
possessions (Luke 9:25; 12:15). All of us receive more from the
bounty of God than we deserve, but we probably do not receive
as much from the bounty of people as we deserve.

Consequently, we react angrily. That reaction can become like
this fox, the little fox that ruins the vineyards in blossom.

Our anger about past hurts will nibble away at our
thoughts and feelings and eventually devour us if we are not
careful. The fox is red. Red is a color, one of those four primary colors we can see in a glass prism.

It is a bold color, easily recognizable. When we are embar-
rassed, we blush red. When we are humiliated, we flush red. When

we believe something is torrid, we say it is red hot.

I have discovered that people play a lot of games. One of the games I played as a child could be called "I Gotcha Last." It was a simple juvenile game without much point except to hit the other person and do it last. You didn't win unless you gave the last lick.

The red fox fits into that game. It might disguise itself under the cloak of anger, malice, retaliation, resentment, bitterness, and maybe even hatred. It is the inner hostility that we allow to build up over a period of time against another person or persons, or maybe even against God.

Yes, even against God! A lot of people are down on God. People who have no one else to blame for their misfortunes will aim their hostility toward God. Many people have bitterness, resentment, and hate—even for God.

So catch us the foxes, the little red foxes that are keeping people out of the kingdom of God. They're destroying the spirit of love and cooperation among those in the kingdom, giving miserable days to those whose tender blossoms they feed upon.

Anger is an emotion that is almost as natural as breathing. It is part of an act of self-preservation. When an animal is hurt or threatened, even a normally mild-mannered animal will strike back. The same can be said for human beings.

Anger occurs in varying degrees of intensity. We can be mildly bothered by something—just enough to take away our peace of mind and bring irritation to our emotions. We can also be so terribly distressed by something that we go into a rage and become destructive to persons or property or both.

Samson was angry when his Philistine father-in-law gave his wife to another man. He caught three hundred foxes, tied torches to their tails, and set them loose in the standing grain of the Philistines. That foxy, fiery rage began a cycle of revenge (Judg. 15).

Anger has been called the chief saboteur of the mind. Milton Layden says that anger

> is a significant factor in the formation of many serious diseases . . . and the leading cause of misery, depression, inefficiency, sickness, accidents, loss of work time and financial loss in industry. . . . No matter what the problem—marital conflict, alcoholism, a child's defiance, nervous or physical disease—elimination of hostility is a key factor in its solution.[8]

Perhaps we can understand something about our anger if we understand more about God's anger and wrath. God became angry—but when? His wrath was directed specifically against those individuals, institutions, and nations whose evil acts and overt expressions of injustice created suffering, death, and deprivation for their victims.

Jesus gave us a vivid picture of the wrath of God.

> The Passover of the Jews was near, and Jesus went up to Jerusalem. In the temple he found people selling cattle, sheep, and doves, and the money changers seated at their tables. Making a whip of cords, he drove all of them out of the temple, both the sheep and the cattle. He also poured out the coins of the money changers and overturned their tables.
>
> —*John 2:13-15*

Two things in this incident tell us something about the anger of God expressed through Jesus: the traders' disdain for holiness, and the temple court where the incident occurred.

The sheep and oxen being sold by the temple traders were supposed to be without spot or blemish, but fraud sometimes occurred. Money changers were taking advantage of pilgrim worshipers who had come from faraway places. The rabbis specified that the temple should accept only certain silver coins of Tyre, so money changers sat in the temple area to exchange currency for a fee, often gouging the worshipers. Then people would pay their temple tax, contribute for the public welfare, and buy animals for sacrifices. Their journeys had been so long that they could not bring sheep and oxen with them.

The traders' disrespect for the house of the Lord and the worship that transpired there became disrespect for the Lord God himself. It was more than Jesus could take. His disciples remembered that it was written, "Zeal for thy house will consume me" (John 2:17). Indeed, that was what happened to Jesus. The Father wanted the temple to be held as solemn and sacred, but it was being treated as common and profane. Christ felt intense anger.

The money changing and trading were taking place in the court of the Gentiles. The prophet Isaiah had called for God's house to be "a house of prayer for all peoples" (56:7). For a long time, the Jewish nation had failed in carrying out God's plan for the ages. They were to be "a light to the nations" (49:6), but instead they withheld the light from the nations. As a token accommodation, Gentiles were allotted a courtyard for their place of worship in the temple complex. Now even that was being spoiled for worship by those who had turned it into a marketplace by their dealing and into "a den of robbers" by their cheating (Mark 11:17; Jer. 7:11).

Jesus represented God's wrath, however, only with prophetic words and actions, not by doing violence to erring persons. He used the whip to drive out the animals, not the people. His moral integrity carried the day, but later he was questioned about his authority for cleansing the temple (Mark 11:28). This conflict with the leaders soon led to Jesus being put to death.

We should not present a picture of God's wrath apart from his grace. James Boice writes,

> On the basis of Christ's death, in which he himself received the full outpouring of God's wrath against sin, those who believed now come to experience not wrath (though we richly deserve it) but grace abounding. This is the day of God's grace. Grace does not eliminate wrath; wrath is still stored up against the unrepentant. But grace does eliminate the necessity for everyone to experience [wrath].[9]

The Old Testament provides an interesting story about a red fox and the damage it inflicted on some tender blossoms.

It all began with a broken promise. Saul was the king of Israel, and in the early years of his kingdom, he made great strides in conquering land for his nation.

Saul conquered a people called the Amorites. He virtually wiped them out, and they begged for mercy. God told Saul to have mercy on them. He promised that he would, but he didn't. Among the Amorites was a smaller tribe known as the Gibeonites. Against the will of God, Saul destroyed most of them.

After Saul died, David became the king. Eventually a famine stalked the land. Crops died, people died, nerves were on edge, and the country was in severe trouble. David asked God, "Why, why is this happening?" God told him that it was because of the sins of Saul. He told David to find the remaining Gibeonites and make some restitution to them. David promised God that he would do this, and he did.

"What can Israel do for you to make peace?" he asked. They responded that they wanted no silver or gold, and they wanted no one to be put to death by David's kingdom.

"Then what do you want?" he asked. Much to his surprise and sorrow, they said, "Give us the sons, the seven sons of Saul."

Alas, here comes the red fox of anger and vengeance. Watch it closely and see the damage it can do and will do before it leaves the vineyard.

Saul's sons were found and delivered to the Gibeonites. They were led up a mountain in a ceremony watched by the people. Seven poles were cut. The boys were impaled on the poles, which then were staked into the ground. The Gibeonites paraded beneath the crosses shouting their abuses until the boys were dead. Their bodies were left on display all summer (2 Sam. 21).

"Why," you ask, "why did these seven boys have to die?" The primary answer is that their father had sinned, and children were being punished for the iniquity of their parents or ancestors from generation to generation (Exod. 20:5). The old proverb was coming true:

> The parents have eaten sour grapes,
> and the children's teeth are set on edge.
> —*Jeremiah 31:29*

Yet even that proverb was countered within the Old Testament (Jer. 31:30; Deut. 24:16). The prophet Ezekiel says, "It is only the person who sins that shall die" (Ezek. 18). Jesus goes even further in rejecting the blame game between generations; he offers forgiveness and sees the opportunity for God's healing works to be revealed (John 9).

You have likely heard someone say, "That boy's no good. I know his old man, and he is no good." On and on it goes. It is sad but true that the children do pay for the sins of their parents.

Parents feeling bitterness and resentment toward life often become child abusers, taking out their hostility on helpless children. Some parents feel bitterness and resentment because of their childhood deprivation, then overly coddle their children, giving them everything they want. They say, "They'll never go without like I had to." Thus many children never learn what it means to be mature, responsible adults.

Some parents have rejected God in their lives because of

bitterness or resentment toward God. They may arrange their lives and family schedules to prevent their children or themselves from having any conscious contact with God.

Catch us the foxes, the little foxes of parental anger and bitterness, hatred and resentment, for these are destroying the tender vines of their children.

"The Gibeonites had harbored bitterness and resentment for so long, and then they had an opportunity for revenge, to kill seven sons of Saul. Revenge is a powerful motive for terrible deeds. No one is immune. Read the Psalms; even there you will find in the holy experiences of the psalmist expressions of revenge: "Destroy all my enemies. . . . Wipe them out. . . . Kill all those who are against me." The red fox is everywhere!

Someone said, "Hating a man is like burning down your own house to get rid of a rat." The one who is bitter and filled with hate often suffers more than the one for whom the bitterness and hatred is intended.

The late C. Roy Angell told about a woman who wanted her husband to buy her a fur coat for $600. The husband rejected her plea on the grounds that they could not afford it. She became so bitter, resentful, and hostile toward him that eventually she became ill and had to have a part of her stomach removed. From her hospital bed, she said, "That ought to teach the old skinflint. I asked him for a $600 fur coat, and now he has to pay a $1,500 doctor bill." Poor dear! He lost the money, she lost part of her stomach, and she thought he lost the most.[10]

Hatred, uncontrolled anger, grudge-bearing, resentments—

all are poisonous to the human mind and body. So catch us the foxes, the little red foxes, and put them to death, for they are destroying our vines.

How can we gain the victory? How did the King deal with that fox? First, let me suggest that we not expect too much from life. I would like to say, "Be kind to others, and they will be kind to you." I'd like to say that, but I can't. Some won't return kindness. Yet kindness is still the best behavior. I'd like to say, "Treat others as you would have them treat you, and that is the way they will treat you" (see Matt. 7:12). I'd like to say that, but I can't. Some will, some won't, but it is still the best way for you to behave.

Injustices, abuses, and rejection are realities in this world. "This is my Father's world," we sing (see Ps. 24:1). But we do not yet see everything in cooperation with God and subject to Christ's reign (Heb. 2:8-9; 1 Cor. 15:24-28). There is a coming judgment, a heaven, and a hell—because some things in this life are unbalanced.

Second, let us not judge a book by its first chapter. The early rejection that one experiences need not be the final story of one's life. Helen Keller, the great saint, was born without sight, without hearing, and without the ability to speak. Later in life she said, "I do not know the meaning of the darkness, but I've learned the overcoming of it." We can make something good happen in spite of those things that might otherwise create a bitter spirit.

Finally, I invite you to surrender to Christ your life, your relationships, and even your excuses for bitterness. He has the wonderful ability to enable you to forgive and to live as if that offense had never happened. The Lord can create within you a clean heart and renew a right spirit within (Ps. 51:10). When you are surrendered to the Lord, you may still receive rejection, abuses, and injustices, but you handle them better. Consequently, you live with more inner peace.

The King can handle the red fox!

FOR REFLECTION

The Red Fox of Anger

Anger is an emotion, an involuntary reaction to a displeasing situation or event. As long as anger is limited to this involuntary, initial emotion, it may be considered a normal reaction. But we respond improperly to anger when we lose our tempers or store it up so it makes us bitter, resentful, or hostile; then it becomes dangerous. It is here that the Bible calls us to account.

Billy Graham writes:

> The Bible does not forbid displeasure, but it sets up two controls. The first is to keep anger clear of bitterness, spite, or hatred. The second is to check daily on whether we have handled malevolent feelings. There is an old Latin proverb, "He who goes angry to bed has the devil for a bedfellow." Of course, there are many irritations in life. They become prime opportunities for Satan to lead us into evil passion.[11]

ENCOURAGEMENT FROM SCRIPTURE

You must understand this my beloved:
let everyone be quick to listen, slow to speak, slow to anger;
for your anger does not produce God's righteousness.

—James 1:19-20

A soft answer turns away wrath,
but a harsh word stirs up anger.

—Proverbs 15:1

But now you must get rid of all such things—anger, wrath,
malice, slander, and abusive language from your mouth.

—Colossians 3:8

A fool gives full vent to anger,
but the wise quietly holds it back.

—Proverbs 29:11

You were taught to put away your former way of life, your
old self, corrupt and deluded by its lusts, and to be renewed
in the spirit of your minds, and to clothe yourselves with the
new self, created according to the likeness of God in true righ-
teousness and holiness.

—Ephesians 4:22-24

CHAPTER FOUR

In Search of the Blue Fox

As a deer longs for the flowing streams,
so my soul longs for you, O God.
My soul thirsts for God, for the living God.
When shall I come and behold the face of God?
My tears have been my food day and night,
while people say to me continually,
"Where is your God?"

These things I remember, as I pour out my soul:
how I went with the throng,
and led them in procession to the house of God,
with glad shouts and songs of thanksgiving,
a multitude keeping festival.
Why are you cast down, O my soul,
and why are you disquieted within me?
Hope in God; for I shall again praise him,
my help and my God.

My soul is cast down within me;
therefore I remember you
from the land of Jordan and of Hermon, from Mount Mizar.
Deep calls to deep at the thunder of your cataracts;
all your waves and your billows have gone over me.
By day the Lord commands his steadfast love,
and at night his song is with me,
a prayer to the God of my life.

I say to God, my rock,
"Why have you forgotten me?
Why must I walk about mournfully
because the enemy oppresses me?"
As with a deadly wound in my body,
my adversaries taunt me,
while they say to me continually,
"Where is your God?"

Why are you cast down, O my soul,
and why are you disquieted within me?
Hope in God; for I shall again praise him,
my help and my God. (Ps. 42)

Take us the foxes,
the little foxes, that spoil the vines;
for our vines have tender grapes.

How do we stay on the top side of life? How do we learn to take the setbacks that life dishes out without being overwhelmed by them? How do we keep from getting depressed? If we are already depressed, how do we overcome it?

This fox is blue. Blue is the color of the sky on a cloudless day. It is the color of the waters on a placid mountain lake. Blue is the color of a thin rim that outlines the snow-capped peaks of the majestic Rockies, and blue is the color of the eyes of many a starry-eyed lover.

Yet, sentimentally and historically we have come to associate this color with melancholy and sadness, as in these lyrics:

> Blue, blue, my world is blue;
> Blue is my world now I'm without you. . . .
>
> I'll have a blue Christmas without you;
> I'll be so blue thinking about you. . . .
>
> I get the blues when it rains,
> The blues I can't lose when it rains. . . .

We talk of "the blues in the night," "the Monday morning blues," and "the washday blues." From the pens of many writers have come lyrics similar to these quoted, accenting the color blue and making it mean despondency, discouragement, and depression.

So, off we go in search of the fox, the little blue fox. It is keeping people out of the kingdom of God because they are not impressed with some of us who claim to be "in." That fox is making life miserable for those whose vines it consumes.

Catch us the foxes, wrote Solomon, the little foxes, that are ruining the vineyards—for our vines have tender blossoms.

May I explode a myth? "When you are a Christian," some say, "all sadness will leave, all discouragement will vanish, and 'every day with Jesus will be sweeter than the day before.' You'll be 'walking in sunlight all of life's journey, over the mountain, through the deep vale.' Troubles? Who needs them? 'We're living on the mountain underneath the cloudless sky; . . . we're drinking at the fountain that never shall run dry.' Oh yes, 'we're feasting on the manna from a bountiful supply, praise God, we're dwelling in Beulah Land.' "

I like the songs. I even like the sentiment they express. I wish I could believe them, but I have lived long enough to know that the lives of all humans follow similar patterns, whether they are Christians or not.

We will not always get what we want. We will not always be successful in our attempts to do something worthwhile. Henry Wadsworth Longfellow said, "Into each life some rain must fall." Defeats, disappointments, sicknesses, and deaths will bring despair and some despondency with them.

Everyone will sin, and sin brings guilt in its wake. Guilt has a depressive quality about it. Everyone will get tired. Tiredness, weariness, and fatigue often make us prey for the little fox, the little blue fox.

Some people of the past were greater believers than

most of us will ever be, and yet they knew the experience of the valley. John Bunyan, author of *Pilgrim's Progress;* Thomas à Kempis, author of *Imitation of Christ;* John Henry Newman, author of the hymn "Lead, Kindly Light"; the prolific writers Charles Lamb and Samuel Johnson; Chopin, the gifted composer of music; and Abraham Lincoln—these all were such sensitive souls that they became vulnerable to the blue mood of depression.

Job was there, expressing a bleak outlook.

> I am allotted months of emptiness,
> and nights of misery are apportioned to me. . . .
> My days are swifter than a weaver's shuttle,
> and come to their end without hope.
>
> —*Job 7:3, 6*

In response to Job's physical and mental condition, his wife finally said, "Curse God, and die" (2:9). Every vestige of God's presence seemed to be gone. No matter where she looked, God seemed to be absent, no longer protecting them. She took it as long as she could. Then because she loved her husband, she thought he would be better off dead than the way he was.

Job was down, but he was not out. "You speak as any foolish woman would speak," he replied. "Shall we receive the good at the hand of God, and not receive the bad?" (2:10). That was the echo of faith that sometimes rings through the yawning chasms of life's deep canyons.

Jeremiah, the great prophet, knew the experience. He

cried out, "Woe is me, my mother, that you ever bore me, a man of strife and contention to the whole land" (15:10).

Though Christians and non-Christians alike are often victims of the valley of depression, Christians have a great plus going for them. They have God and the multitude of those who praise God.

No one knows all of the causes of depression. Doctors don't, psychiatrists and psychologists don't. Counselors, including ministers, admit that they cannot fully explain it.

The sixteenth-century theologian John of the Cross described it in his book entitled *The Dark Night of the Soul*. Sometimes we naively order those who are depressed, "Snap out of it!" But that's like asking dogs to fly. If they could, they would. No one truly enjoys that miserable, unhappy feeling. But like a sly fox, it creeps up on us.

Depression can come on the wings of memory, the lingering taste of a past failure or bad experience. Everything can be moving along smoothly. Nothing is troubling the water. Then the mind with its uncanny capacity to recall can flash a thought into our consciousness and totally erase our present joy.

Sometimes it comes on the heels of some great victory, some high moment of spiritual exhilaration. Who knows when it will show up? Who knows how to prevent it?

The clearest picture of the blue fox in the Bible is the fox that was eating at Elijah's tender blossoms. When I study Elijah's life, I understand both the fox and the King who destroys the fox much better.

On Mt. Carmel, Elijah was revved up. He had had enough of Baalism. He was tired of seeing the people bowing to worship Baal, a pagan god. So he called for a showdown on Mt. Carmel. Elijah was nauseated with the wishy-washy ways of the Israelites, who were holding to God with one hand and to idolatry with the other, "limping between two different opinions" (1 Kings 18).

The prophets of Baal called for response from their god by cutting themselves with lances and swords. They were begging through the noonday and into the afternoon for their god to flash fire on the altar. It didn't happen.

When Elijah's opportunity came, he prayed earnestly for a response from heaven. He did not have a chance to finish his prayer. Fire rained from the sky and ignited the water-drenched wood and altar; it even dried out the ground around it. It was a magnificent hour for this faithful prophet. God had honored his faith and daring by supplying him with an answer to his prayer. Had it not happened, he would no doubt have been slain on the hillside.

The people repented. The prophets of Baal fled, and some were slain. The crowds began to cheer, "The Lord indeed is God. The Lord indeed is God!" But, alas, here comes the fox; watch it closely. It came through the words of the wicked queen, Jezebel. She said, "I'll have that prophet's head" (1 Kings 19:2).

So Elijah ran away. He fled a hundred miles to the south

and then ran a full day's journey into the wilderness. Exhausted and depressed, he said, "It is enough; now, O Lord, take away my life, for I am no better than my ancestors" (19:4). One can hardly imagine that this could be the same person as the bold prophet of the Lord on Mt. Carmel.

What happened? In his case, a number of things produced depression. First, there was a letdown after a greatly anticipated event. The same thing can happen to a new mother. She has carried the developing child in her womb for nine months and has accommodated herself to its needs. Then, upon giving birth, a letdown feeling can come to her. It is not a disappointed feeling. She is physically tired and feels depression that may be psychologically induced or due to changes in body chemistry.

A child can experience a tremendous day at the amusement park. Yet when the day is over, he may have a melancholy disposition. He may not know why he is sad. Elijah had gotten "up" for the occasion. His adrenalin was flowing through his body. Then it was over. God had won a great victory through him. But he became depressed, and his adrenalin was used up.

Second, all of us have a basic loneliness. There is an inner sanctum in the soul of each individual that no one knows but God and that person, who does not even fully know what is going on. Paul said, "All must carry their own loads" (Gal. 6:5). He knew that there are things that we cannot share with another human being. We must walk some valleys alone. Only God can walk with us.

In Elijah's case, he was a loner. He wasn't married. He didn't seem to be close to any family or to any other human being. In fact, he thought he was the only person in all of the world who felt as strongly as he did about God (1 Kings 19:10, 14). He needed to confide in someone. We all need someone who will weep with us when we weep and laugh with us when we laugh (Rom. 12:15). If we lack such friends, depression is more likely to visit us.

Thus Elijah, let down and lonely, did the next thing people do when they become depressed. He tried a change of environment.

We sometimes try a new location, a change of jobs, and adjusted circumstances. "I've got to get out of this room, away from this house, away from this place." Some people try a change of companions. Elijah fled to another place, a place where he would be alone again.

He was tired, so very tired that he despaired of life itself. "I just want to die," he said (1 Kings 19:4). People sometimes give up or even feel suicidal when death seems to be a more pleasant prospect than their physical circumstances.

Isn't it wonderful that God can and often does meet us in the valley? The King knows our frame. "He remembers that we are dust" (Ps. 103:14). Physically, we get tired, run-down, exhausted, fatigued. God caused a deep sleep to come upon Elijah. God understands our bodies better than we do.

When the prophet awakened, there was food baking on

hot stones and a jar of water provided for his thirst (1 Kings 19:5-6). Was God recognizing the fact that our physical needs can prevent a clear view of the larger reality? I think so.

Afterward, he took Elijah to a place where some natural phenomena were happening: devastating winds were bending the trees, a fire was burning out of control, and an earthquake shook the ground beneath his feet. "The world is bigger than you are," God seemed to be saying. "Stop the winds if you can! Extinguish the fire if you're able! Control the quaking of the earth!" The King knows that sometimes we take ourselves too seriously. We have a tendency to forget that there is awesome power beyond our own. The God who could control nature could surely look after the details of a despairing prophet's life.

Finally, Elijah heard a voice, a still, quiet voice. "What are you doing here, Elijah?" God asked. It was worship. The wilderness became a sanctuary. Elijah, who had been so busy feeding others, was fed. "Elijah," God said, "my work is larger than one man, larger than life itself. After you're gone, it will still go on. Go and find Elisha. He is waiting to be anointed as a prophet." Self-pity goes hand-in-hand with depression, so God helped Elijah to get his mind off himself and on to a continuing movement of salvation history.

The Lord God also told Elijah

> Yet I will leave seven thousand in Israel,
> all the knees that have not bowed to Baal,
> and every mouth that has not kissed him.
> —1 Kings 19:18

Elijah had a whole congregation of people to meet, the faithful who shared in keeping the covenant with the Lord God. They would strengthen him in dealing with the blue fox of depression.

We who are depressed need the fellowship of faithful friends and the help of wise counselors and doctors. They can listen to us talk through our concerns. Physicians can test our body to see if there is a chemical imbalance. Counselors can test our soul to find any spiritual block. We may be sabotaging ourselves by false perceptions and self-defeating inner dialogue. We need God's truth.

In Psalm 43:3-5 of *The Living Bible,* we read words of encouragement and promise.

> Oh, send out your light and your truth—let them lead me.
> Let them lead me to your Temple on your holy mountain, Zion.
> There I will go to the altar of God, my exceeding joy,
> and praise him with my harp.
> O God—my God!
>
> O my soul, why be so gloomy and discouraged?
> Trust in God!
> I shall again praise him for his wondrous help;
> he will make me smile again,
> for he is my God!

Yes, Christians have the right to get depressed, but not to stay that way. When believers stay depressed, they keep others out of the kingdom of God; they bear false witness to

God's sustaining love.

> As a deer longs for flowing streams,
> so my soul longs for you, O God.

FOR REFLECTION

The Blue Fox of Depression

Depression is possibly responsible for more pain and distress than any other affliction of humankind. Depression has been defined as an emotional condition, either neurotic or psychotic, characterized by feelings of hopelessness, inadequacy, gloominess, dejection, sadness, difficulty in thinking and concentration, and inactivity.

Depression may be a reaction to adverse situations, defeats, or setbacks—such as a death in the family, a rebellious son or daughter, or loss of employment.

Depression may come because of spiritual disobedience and unresolved sin involving anger and bitterness, jealousy, grudges, a divorce, or immorality.

Depression may be the result of persons setting standards and goals they cannot attain. This may be true for both economic or spiritual goals; failure brings on depression.

Corrie ten Boom often quoted these words:

> Look within and be depressed;
> Look without and be distressed;
> Look at Jesus and be at rest.[12]

ENCOURAGEMENT FROM SCRIPTURE

Surely he has borne our infirmities and carried our diseases; yet we accounted him stricken, struck down by God, and afflicted. But he was wounded for our transgressions, crushed for our iniquities; upon him was the punishment that made us whole, and by his bruises we are healed.
—Isaiah 53:4-5

We are afflicted in every way, but not crushed; perplexed, but not driven to despair; persecuted, but not forsaken; struck down, but not destroyed.
—2 Corinthians 4:8-9

It is no longer I who live, but it is Christ who lives in me. And the life I now live in the flesh I live by faith in the Son of God, who loved me and gave himself for me.
—Galatians 2:20

The human spirit will endure sickness; but a broken spirit—who can bear?
—Proverbs 18:14

Trust in the Lord with all your heart, and do not rely on your own insight. In all your ways acknowledge him, and he will make straight your paths.
—Proverbs 3:5-6

CHAPTER FIVE

In Search of the Green Fox

Someone in the crowd said to him, "Teacher, tell my brother to divide the family inheritance with me." But he said to him, "Friend, who set me to be a judge or arbitrator over you?" And he said to them, "Take care! Be on your guard against all kinds of greed; for one's life does not consist in the abundance of possessions." Then he told them a parable: "The land of a rich man produced abundantly. And he thought to himself, 'What should I do, for I have no place to store my crops?' Then he said, 'I will do this: I will pull down my barns, and build larger ones, and there I will store all my grain and my goods. And I will say to my soul, "Soul, you have ample goods laid up for many years; relax, eat, drink, and be merry!" ' But God said to him, 'You fool! This very night your soul is being demanded of you. And the things you have prepared, whose will they be?' So it is with those who store up treasures for themselves but are not rich toward God." (Luke 12:13-21)

Take us the foxes,
the little foxes, that spoil the vines:
for our vines have tender grapes.

How do we cope with the inequities in life? Life is unequal, we know. All persons are not created equal. As George Orwell said in *Animal Farm*, all are created equal, but some are "more equal than others." Some are prettier than others. Some seem to float through life without needing to put forth much effort. Some are healthier than others. Some are wealthier than others. How do you handle that, especially if you are on the minus side of the ledger?

Green is a color. It is the color of a well-kept lawn even in the middle of a hot summer. It is the color of deep pools of water in the shade of a giant oak tree. Green is the color of trees deep in the forest. Green is the color of some people's eyes. Green is the color of some insects and reptiles and fish.

Solomon said, "Catch us the foxes, the little foxes that ruin the vineyards—for our vineyards are in blossom." There is a fox eating at the vines of many of us and spoiling our happiness and productivity. Though small in size, it can grow and become a consuming beast. It can devour one's life and leave a mere specimen of the former self—cold, callous, unloved, and unloving.

Day after day is ruined by its nibbling; sleepless nights are spent in tossing and turning because of its damage. Still, we pamper it, pet it, and feed it. We expect it to go away, but it doesn't. We should be not deceived. Wherever any animal is being fed, that is where it will stay. Why leave?

This fox is green. It is green with envy, green with jealousy. It is green with greed and green with covetousness. It will drive its victims to insane levels of conduct to achieve their goals. It has caused many people endless heartaches and has destroyed entire families.

The fox is green with jealously, but all jealousy is not bad. On Mount Sinai Moses heard God say, "You shall have no other gods before me, . . . for I the Lord your God am a jealous God" (Exod. 20:3-5). There is an unselfish kind of jealousy. It is a jealousy that is totally interested in the well-being of another individual. It looks out for another's welfare.

Such is the jealousy that God expresses. In effect, God was saying to the people, "I want the very best for you. I don't want you to get caught up in idol worship because idols are empty and unreal. They have no capacity to reward you or relate to you in ways that will bring ultimate fulfillment to you."

Later, God inspired Paul to say that "the present form of this world is passing away" (1 Cor. 7:31). It stands to reason, then, that a person who builds an entire life on something that is changing, that is vanishing, stands a great chance of losing self and happiness.

There are many places where that is applicable. God wants us to have healthy relationships with others. We love our families, we love our friends, but we don't depend on them as we are to depend on God alone. People die, people move away, people fail; if people have become "gods" to us, we will be left without a foundation when people change. That is why God told us to have no other gods before him. The Lord knows how desolate life can be when a person has lost a god.

The jealousy God has for us is a healthy jealousy for it is totally selfless. It was best expressed in the coming of Christ to be our Savior. As Paul wrote:

> And being found in human form,
> [Christ] humbled himself
> and became obedient to the point of death—
> even death on a cross.
> —*Philippians 2:7-8*

A Savior who is willing to do that for people is certainly not jealous for selfish reasons.

When Paul wrote to the church at Corinth, he said,

> I feel a divine jealousy for you,
> for I promised you in marriage to one husband,
> to present you as a chaste virgin to Christ.
> But I am afraid that as the serpent deceived Eve
> by its cunning,
> your thoughts will be led astray
> from a sincere and pure devotion to Christ.
> —*2 Corinthians 11:2*

Believers *ought* to be fully dedicated to God, striving first for God's reign and his righteousness (Matt. 6:24, 33). Parents *ought* to be jealous over their children, looking out for them, interested in them, giving them the best they have in the discipline of the Lord (Eph. 6:1-4). Citizens ought to look out for the best interests of their country, giving to it what is due (Mark 12:17; Rom. 13:7). But in these cases, *jealousy* means self-giving concern and love for others.

However, there is a jealousy to be shunned. It is the perversion of love, excessively possessive, obsessive, and selfish. It does not say, "I want the best for you for your sake"; it says, "I want the best for you for *my* sake."

We feel it when our friends give to others some of the affection and attention we crave for ourselves. We are jealous when others get the admiration we want. Undoubtedly, our cravings for *p*osition, for *p*restige, or for *p*ower can become the seedbeds that foster this jealous spirit, the *p*'s that feed this pesky fox.

All of us have certain ideas of what life should be, how it should work out, what we should receive from it. Often life doesn't happen that way; we fail, we lose, others get the honors, the glory, and the crown. Then the green fox of jealousy eats vigorously at our vines. We become filled with hate toward the ones we blame for our failures. Many people cultivate this spirit in business, politics, sports, and love life.

What are the symptoms of the green fox's activity? Jealous people sometimes tell lies about other people. They are quick to gossip about the faults and failings of others. They are most adept at the critical spirit. Some even resort to murder. What a beast the green fox is!

Charles Swindoll speaks from experience when he talks about jealousy.

> Jealousy will decimate a friendship, dissolve a romance, and destroy a marriage. It will shoot tension through the ranks of professionals. It will nullify unity on a team, . . . ruin a church, . . . separate preachers, . . . foster competition in a choir, bringing bitterness and finger-pointing among talented instrumentalists and capable singers.
>
> With squint eyes, jealousy will question motives and deplore another's success. It will become severe, suspicious, narrow, and negative.[13]

The fox is also green with greed and covetousness. The word *covet* means "to desire, to long for, to crave that which belongs to another." One writer calls it "inordinate desire," disordered, lacking restraint.

We covet the property of others, even the companions of others. We covet others' positions of leadership, their popularity. We even covet the appearance of others. We sometimes call it "keeping up with the Joneses."

This fox is found in respectable Wall Street offices and in humble mountain hamlets. It is present in the classroom as well as in marketing and other business enterprises. It is on the football field and in the choir. It is in the Sunday school classroom and the ministry.

One must be careful not to mistake covetousness for ambition. On the surface, they look much the same. Ambition to carry out constructive goals is good, it is human, it is divine. The world is a better place for us all because of it.

An ambitious man developed the incandescent lamp and the phonograph. An ambitious man perfected the telephone. Ambitious people developed the horseless carriage.

Such ambition is the springboard from which we leap into life to do whatever we feel God has equipped us to do. Financial success, leadership success, recognition for what we're doing—who of us would deny that we have some of this blood flowing through our veins? Nor is it bad!

However, what is bad is the way we sometimes stretch for these unreachable stars. Covetousness is not far removed from ambition. It is difficult to tell where one ends and the other begins. It is easier to look behind and see where ambition became coveting than to look ahead and see where it is going to happen.

The green fox eats at our tender blossoms until we crave the money, the success, the power, the recognition that another has, and we are consumed by our jealousy and covetousness.

One of the worst consequences of jealousy is that it blinds us to the finer things in life. We can become so obsessed with our goals that we lose sight of the way we're getting there and the price we're paying en route.

How many marriages have been dissolved because a workaholic husband is determined to get ahead, whatever that means to him? How many children have become virtual orphans because of the obsession of their parents to reach some lofty plateau they have set for themselves? How much hate is engendered toward those who seem to have made it? How much inner disruption of peace have people experienced because they could not have what others seem to have?

Covetousness creates feelings that depend upon the changing, shifting sands of life. We could do without many things if we were forced to do so. Coveting makes people discontent with life as it is.

Whether we agree with their actions or not, the flower children of the 1960s were saying something significant to us when they made nontraditional choices about clothes and money and went out into the backwoods to adopt a simple lifestyle. Perhaps they were reminding us that there are some things more important than fighting and scratching to reach the top, crying and fussing, and destroying human personality on the way.

Covetousness leads to all kinds of wrongdoing. When the lights went out one night in New York City, looters had a field day because they coveted what they couldn't afford to buy. Murder, adultery, character defamation, and much more can come from the work of the green fox.

Furthermore, coveting blinds us to human need. It can change a normally caring person into a graspy, greedy individual, cold and heartless. It causes some to want to hold others down because they cannot feel superior unless there are others who are inferior.

So catch us the foxes, the little green foxes that are making life miserable for us poor humans who measure success in terms of money possessed and positions occupied. They're keeping many people out of the kingdom of God.

The King can help rid our fields of this fox. He reminds us that "life does not consist in the abundance of possessions." "Vanity of vanities," shouted the Old Testament teacher who had experienced life's good material things but found them to be empty of any lasting significance (Eccles. 1:2).

The King still asks, "What will it profit them to gain the whole world and forfeit their life? Indeed, what can they give in return for their life?" (Mark 8:36-37).

The green fox is no match for the King. I know of only one way to be rid of that fox. It comes in a surrender of our lives to the lordship of Jesus Christ. Our thoughts and actions will not be any better than our spirits, and Christ can change us from the inside out.

For your sake, don't let the green fox keep you out of the kingdom of God. For God's sake, don't let the green fox cause you to keep others out.

FOR REFLECTION

The Green Fox of Envy, Jealousy, and Covetousness

Envy, jealousy, and covetousness are interrelated evils. Discontentment with our positions and possessions often indicates a self-centered attitude which leads to intolerant, resentful, and even malicious feelings toward a real or imagined rival. We may covet the success, personality, material possessions, good looks, or position of another. Then, to compensate for a frustrated ego, we make unkind and destructive remarks and submerge ourselves in self-pity, anger, bitterness, and depression.

The apostle Paul gives the all-time antidote to the sins of envy, jealousy, and covetousness.

> I know what it is to have little,
> and I know what it is to have plenty.
> In any and all circumstances I have learned the secret
> of being well-fed and of going hungry,
> of having plenty and of being in need.
> I can do all things through him who strengthens me.
> —*Philippians 4:12-13*

ENCOURAGEMENT FROM SCRIPTURE

So if you have been raised with Christ, seek the things that are above, where Christ is, seated at the right hand of God. Set your minds on things that are above, not on things that are on earth, for you have died, and your life is hidden with Christ in God. When Christ who is your life is revealed, then you also will be revealed with him in glory.

—Colossians 3:1-4

*A tranquil mind gives life to the flesh,
but passion makes the bones rot.*

—Proverbs 14:30

Keep your lives free from the love of money, and be content with what you have; for he has said, I will never leave you or forsake you.

—Hebrews 13:5

And let us consider how to provoke one another to love and good deeds, not neglecting to meet together, as is the habit of some, but encouraging one another, and all the more as you see the Day approaching.

—Hebrews 10:24-25

CHAPTER SIX

In Search of the Yellow Fox

I t is as if a man going on a journey summoned his slaves and entrusted his property to them; to one he gave five talents, to another two, to another one, to each according to his ability. Then he went away. The one who had received the five talents went off at once and traded with them, and made five more talents. In the same way, the one who had the two talents made two more talents. But the one who had received the one talent went off and dug a hole in the ground and hid his master's money. After a long time, the master of those slaves came and settled accounts with them. Then the one who had received the five talents came forward, bringing five more talents, saying, "Master, you handed over to me five talents; see I have made five more talents." His master said to him, "Well done, good and trustworthy slave; you have been trustworthy in a few things, I will put you in charge of many things; enter into the joy of your master!" And the one with the two talents also came forward, saying, "Master, you handed over to me two talents; see, I have made two more talents." His master said to him, "Well done, good and trustworthy slave; you have been trustworthy in a few things, I will put you in charge of many things; enter into the joy of your master." Then the one who had received the one talent also came forward, saying, "Master, I knew that you were a harsh man, reaping where you did not sow, and gathering where you did not scatter seed; so I was afraid, and I went and hid your talent in the ground. Here you have what is yours." But his master replied, "You wicked and lazy slave! You knew, did you not, that I reap where I did not sow, and gather where I did not scatter? Then you ought to have invested my money with the bankers, and on my return I would have received what was my own with interest. So take the talent from him, and give it to the one with the ten talents. For to all those who have, more will be given, and they will have an abundance; but from those who have nothing, even what they have will be taken away. As for this worthless slave, throw him into the outer darkness, where there will be weeping and gnashing of teeth." (Matt. 25:14-30)

> Take us the foxes,
> the little foxes, that spoil the vines;
> for our vines have tender grapes.

For the first time, a little boy was taken to a church worship service by his father. He listened intently to the minister, who was telling a story about a man who had been crucified. The boy became upset to think that a good man like that would be put to death. However, something bothered him more than that: as he looked around, no one else seemed to be concerned at all. No one had tears in their eyes. No one seemed to be surprised. No one appeared to care that it had happened.

The lad began to cry. When his father heard the child weeping, he turned and muttered angrily, "Don't take it to heart. Someone will think you're strange."

Strange—to be alive and sensitive? The proud philosophers of Athens said the good news about Jesus was strange (Acts 17:18-21). Believers were thought to be strange because they didn't join in drunken revels (1 Pet. 4:4).

It takes courage to live different from the sins of society. Brave people are willing to show their colors, to declare their allegiance to Christ, even if others think them strange. They are not yellow.

This fox is yellow. Yellow is a color, and it can be a gorgeous one. When it is soft and mild, it is easy to look at. It invites you to touch it.

However, yellow is a color we associate with cowardice and timidity. In athletics, we say that a person who cringes before an opponent "has a yellow streak up his back." We mean that he is afraid. He is a coward.

So catch us the foxes, the little yellow foxes. They are eating at the tender blossoms of our lives and causing many of us to bear false witness for Christ.

The yellow fox was at work on the plains just across the river from Canaan. Moses selected twelve leaders and said,

"Go up and look at the land that the Lord our God will deliver to us, and return to make your report." When they returned, the majority reported, "Great! It's a great land, beautiful and fruitful." But the majority also complained, "It's occupied by giants; we can't conquer it. In fact, we will seem like grasshoppers to them" (based on Num. 13).

The yellow fox appeared in the garden of Gethsemane the night the armed guards showed up to make their arrest. Jesus stood alone. His disciples had fled for their lives. Peter stood with him for awhile, but soon he denied Christ and ran away, too (Mark 14).

The yellow fox was in New York City the night a woman was stabbed thirty-eight times by her assailant. She screamed for help, she cried out in pain. The lights went on in a nearby apartment building. Windows were raised, but no one helped Kitty Genovese. In fact, no one even bothered to call the police.

Under the control of the yellow fox, one might change a beatitude (Matt. 5:9) to say, "Blessed are the peacekeepers, for they do not have to face the tension of controversy. Blessed are the keepers of the status quo, for they shall not pay the price of daring adventure, even the adventure of faith."

One writer said, "Jesus Christ was not crucified on a communion table between two candlesticks. He was crucified outside the walls of a great city between two thieves" (see Heb. 13:12). Christ would not have been there had he listened to the yellow fox: "You saved others, now save yourself" (based on Mark 15:29-32). Many of us play the popular game of saving ourselves. It isn't hazardous to our health; it takes little if any real skill; and what's more, it's convenient, expedient, and comfortable.

On the other hand, real commitment demands that we get in the trenches, become dirty in spiritual warfare, perhaps scarred, and marked with the wounds of the Lord Jesus. In the end, the Master will say, "Well done! You've fought a good fight; you've finished the course; you've kept the faith" (see 2 Tim. 4:7).

Why is the yellow fox so effective? It might begin with a mistaken idea that the Christian is a scared individual who mostly counts beads, sings hymns, blesses the beggars, and minds the business of the organized church.

There is an old proverb you may have heard:

> Never trouble trouble, till trouble troubles you,
> or else you'll double trouble, and trouble others too.

Obviously there is some meaning and truth to that bit of wisdom. We certainly don't want to stir up a brew of trouble, like the witches in Shakespeare's *Macbeth:*

> Double, double toil and trouble;
> Fire burn and cauldron bubble.

But what would our world be today if everyone had adhered to that philosophy?

Suppose Moses had not bothered Pharaoh: there would have been no exodus, no Promised Land. Suppose Martin

Luther had never challenged the Roman Church: there would have been no Reformation, no renewal in the church. In both cases, God could have worked out his purposes in other ways, but it might have taken longer, and we wouldn't remember Moses or Luther.

In the United States, if Susan Brownell Anthony and Elizabeth Cady Staunton had not challenged the voting rules, women might have waited many more years to claim their right to vote. If Martin Luther King had not troubled the status quo in race relations, the blacks might still be second-class citizens.

Henry David Thoreau, who marched to the beat of a different drummer, was put into prison because he dared to take a stand against what he felt was an injustice in the government. Ralph Waldo Emerson visited him and asked, "Why, Henry, what are you doing in there?" Thoreau responded, "Nay, Ralph, that is not the question: The question is, What are you doing out there?"

People who take risks are often rewarded with pain and deprivation.

John Gillespie Magee Jr. wrote about an experience he had while flying. His poem expresses his daring, risking his life for something he thought important.

> Oh, I have slipped the surly bonds of earth,
> And danced the skies on laughter-silvered wings.
> Sunward I've climbed, and joined the tumbling mirth
> Of sun-split clouds—and done a hundred things
> You have not dreamed of—wheeled and soared and swung

High in the sunlit silence. Hov'ring there,
I've chased the shouting wind along, and flung
My eager craft through footless halls of air.
Up, up the long, delirious, burning blue,
I've topped the wind-swept heights with easy grace
Where never lark, or even eagle flew—
And, while with silent, lifting mind I've trod
The high, untrespassed sanctity of space,
Put out my hand and touched the face of God.[14]

However, many of us have never put out our hands and "touched the face of God." We're landlocked, earthbound, timid, and afraid. We bury our talents instead of investing them. We save our lives and end up losing them.

Suppose God had never challenged Satan. There would have been no Bethlehem, no carpenter shop, no good Samaritan, no Calvary, no Easter, no hope.

We will always take risks when we dare to do mighty things.

As Teddy Roosevelt believed,

Far better it is to dare mighty things, to win glorious triumphs, even though checkered by failure, then to take rank with those poor spirits who neither enjoy much nor suffer much because they live in the gray twilight that knows neither victory nor defeat.[15]

There are others, of course, who believe that the Christian should be a person of commitment, of involvement, but they never take it personally. Whether that is due to laziness, lack of time, or lack of commitment, the result is still the same. Taking on responsibility involves learning. Knowing something often demands a response. If we remain uninvolved, we let others carry responsibility which God may want us to take.

There are some who want to get involved, to be committed, but they are afraid of failure. Paul Tournier said, "The fear of not succeeding is, for many people, the biggest obstacle in their way. It holds them back from trying anything at all. And for lack of trying, they never give themselves a chance of succeeding."[16]

Fear—what a paralyzing emotion it is! It keeps some people on the sidelines, not in the game. It keeps others just at the edge of real fulfillment. Some are afraid to fall in love for fear that they will be hurt. Some are afraid to express their true emotions and commitment for fear that they will be laughed at or even rejected.

Whatever the cause of such fear, the result is the same. No contribution is made, so no fulfillment is experienced. No investment is made, so no gain is received. No risk is taken; therefore, no victory is won.

William Dyal expressed this thought:

> Courage dies . . . in mediocrity. Tacitus described Tiberius, the Roman Emperor: "He feared the best, was ashamed of the worst, and chose the innocuous middle." Life . . . does not have to end here. Such should not be the final word. Even though trial, despair, and finally death marked the course of the Apostle Paul, there was a different spirit about him. He was no god, but he invested his life with courage.[17]

Where do we get that courage? If we are to be free to serve, we must learn to cut the ropes that bind and inhibit us.

Someone said, "Courage is fear that has said its prayers." Paul tells us, "Work out your own salvation with fear and trembling; it is God who is at work in you" (Phil. 2:13).

Eleanor Roosevelt calls us to look fear in the face:

> You gain strength, courage, and confidence by every experience in which you really stop to look fear in the face. You are able to say to yourself, "I lived through this horror. I can take the next thing that comes along.". . . *You must do the thing you think you cannot do.*[18]

Everyone has some inner fears. The difference between the hero and the coward is in what they do with their fears.

"I was afraid," said the third man in Christ's parable of the talents. "I was afraid, so I hid the talent in the ground." Think about that! His life's work was nothing more than a hole in the ground, where he tried to protect what he had been given. It didn't work!

The yellow fox must be hunted down. It must be slain because God commands it. "Seek those things which are above and not the things which are below" (based on Col. 3:2). "Seek them," as Peter Marshall so eloquently said it, "as the needle seeks the pole, as the sunflowers seeks the sun, as the river seeks the sea, as the eagle seeks the ceiling of the world." Such concentration of purpose will help us overcome fears about things on earth.

Think not that the purpose of life is simply to enjoy yourself, have a good time, make money, and live in ease and comfort.

Jesus said, "Foxes have holes, and birds of the air have nests; but the Son of Man has nowhere to lay his head. . . . [Come and] follow me!" (Luke 9:58-59). Jesus tells us, "Do not fear those who kill the body but cannot kill the soul; rather fear him who can destroy both soul and body in hell" (Matt. 10:28). Keeping priorities straight will put fear in its place and give us the courage to go on, trusting and serving God.

We do need to relax, recreate, and refresh our spirits. But life's coffee breaks must never become a substitute for the main business of living.

The yellow fox must be slain because our times demand it. Our world situation makes the yellow fox a dangerous enemy to us all. Failure to dare, to dream, to think high thoughts, to act bravely, to be God's courageous person—such failure might bring fatal results.

All of us need beliefs that make us bold. We must "take every thought captive to obey Christ" (2 Cor. 10:5). One night Jesus met his friends in the upper room. It was a time of great stress and confusion. He spoke about the meaning of his life. "The Son of Man is to be betrayed into human hands, and they will kill him, and three days after being killed, he will rise again" (Mark 9:31).

The disciples did not understand what Jesus was saying and were afraid to ask. The disciples never seemed to hear Jesus' words about the resurrection promise. Isn't that like us? Something can hit us so hard at the beginning of a sentence that we can't stick around long enough to hear the rest of the conversation. All the disciples heard were those dreadful words about Jesus being killed.

Then the time arrived. Jesus said, "Do not let your hearts be troubled. Believe in God, believe also in me" (John 14:1).

One who believes in God and in Jesus Christ has the remedy for a troubled heart and becomes willing to take risks for God's reign. If we truly believe that God can handle every situation in our lives, we are on our way to conquering our fears and destroying the yellow fox.

I wonder if many of us will someday reach a point in our Christian experience when we will lament the fact that we did not do more for our Savior. We will regret that we did not take enough responsibility for sharing his love, for taking a stand against some evil. We'll perhaps wish we could go back and do it over again, *but we can't go back.* We can't change the past. But we can change the future, with God's help.

For your sake, don't let the yellow fox keep you out of the kingdom of God. For God's sake, don't let that fox cause you to keep others out.

FOR REFLECTION

The Yellow Fox of Fear

A moderate sense of fear is normal, even healthy. Fear may be an awareness of impending danger, a defense mechanism. It may just be the pounding heart, flushed face, and sweaty palms in anticipation of being called on in class or asked to make a speech at a meeting. Fears may be reactions to imagined or real circumstances. They can be acute or chronic. Many fearful people tend to infect others with their anxieties and tensions.

Billy Graham writes, "Jesus said we are not to fear; we are not to be anxious; we are not to fret; we are not to worry. The Bible teaches that this type of fear is sin."[19]

Jesus promises,

> Peace I leave with you; my peace I give to you. . . .
> Do not let your hearts be troubled,
> and do not let them be afraid.
> —*John 14:27*

The fear of God is the only fear that conquers all other fears.

ENCOURAGEMENT FROM SCRIPTURE

I sought the Lord, and he answered me,
and he delivered me from all my fears.
> —Psalm 34:4

Strive first for the kingdom of God and his righteousness, and all these things will be given to you as well. So do not worry about tomorrow, for tomorrow will bring worries of its own. Today's trouble is enough for today.
> —Matthew 6:33-34

Do not worry about anything, but in everything by prayer and supplication with thanksgiving let your requests be made known to God. And the peace of God, which surpasses all understanding, will guard your hearts and your minds in Christ Jesus.

—Philippians 4:6-7

Cast all your anxiety on him, because he cares for you.

—1 Peter 5:7

Why are you cast down, O my soul,
and why are you so disquieted within me?
Hope in God, for I shall again praise him,
my help and my God.

—Psalm 42:5

CHAPTER SEVEN

In Search of the Black Fox

You who live in the shelter of the Most High,
who abide in the shadow of the Almighty,
will say to the Lord, "My refuge and my fortress;
my God, in whom I trust."
For he will deliver you from the snare of the fowler
and from the deadly pestilence;
he will cover you with his pinions,
and under his wings you will find refuge;
his faithfulness is a shield and buckler.
You will not fear the terror of the night,
or the arrow that flies by day,
or the pestilence that stalks in darkness,
or the destruction that wastes at noonday.

A thousand may fall at your side,
ten thousand at your right hand;
but it will not come near you.
You will only look with your eyes

and see the punishment of the wicked.

Because you have made the Lord your refuge,
the Most High your dwelling place,
no evil shall befall you,
no scourge come near your tent.

For he will command his angels concerning you
to guard you in all your ways.
On their hands they will bear you up,
so that you will not dash your foot against a stone.
You will tread on the lion and the adder,
the young lion and the serpent
you will trample under foot.

Those who love me, I will deliver;
I will protect those who know my name.
When they call to me, I will answer them;
I will be with them in trouble,
I will rescue them and honor them
With long life I will satisfy them,
and show them my salvation. *(Ps. 91)*

Take us the foxes,
the little foxes, that spoil the vines;
for our vines have tender grapes.

Down in the human heart, Crushed by the tempter,
Feelings lie buried which grace can restore.

—Fanny J. Crosby

Dead, entombed in the dark underground of the soul. The feelings were murdered by the black fox of discouragement and doubt. It is sly and cunning, this pesky animal. It takes advantage of us when we are weak.

This fox is no respecter of person, age, or circumstance, although he does his worst damage to those in the middle of life, the so-called prime of life. No one escapes his meddlesome nibbling and damaging work.

Black is an appropriate color for this fox because black is the color we commonly associate with death. Black is the border marking a column of daily news about accidental death on the highway. Black is the color of the skull placed on a container to warn that the contents are poisonous. Black is the color traditionally worn when mourning someone who has died.

Black is not a color found in the rainbow which God placed in the sky, making a covenant with mankind following the flood. Black is never seen in the glass prism; it is not a pure color. Indeed, black is the absorption of all colors, thus eliminating them and leaving a dark spot where they once were.

Hence, black is the fox which takes all of the color out of life. In its wake it leaves dreams unfulfilled, enthusiasm shipwrecked, and idealism crushed. At its worst it destroys one's will to live. If discouraged persons do not commit suicide, they may drift through life apathetic, cynical, disconnected. Their theme song will be "Vanity of vanities. . . . All is vanity and vexation of spirit, a chasing after wind" (Eccles. 1:2; 2:17, KJV/NRSV). Their poetry is from Shakespeare: "[Life] is a tale told by an idiot, full of sound and fury, signifying nothing" (*Macbeth*).

A person whose vines are badly damaged by the black fox looks at the birth of a newborn baby and exclaims, "Poor thing." At the wedding of starry-eyed lovers, the person outfoxed by this black fox says, "I feel sorry for them." When confronted with an expression of youthful idealism, such a person remarks, "Stick around, kid, you'll get over it. You'll settle down just like the rest of us. Eventually you'll see that life is a survival of the fittest—everyone for self or you'll get crushed beneath the juggernaut of life."

The inscription on many gravestones could well read: "Died at 25; buried at 65." Society is filled with discouraged people who have given up the struggle. They are tired before the end of life's day, victims of the black fox. This is spiritual "destruction that wastes at noonday" (Ps. 91:6).

Once again, let us mount the horses and go with the King in search of the black fox.

Catch us the foxes, the little black foxes, that blight the vineyards and kill off the tender blossoms.

The black fox is an opportunist who takes advantage of

human frailty. Failure in business, the loss of health, a shattered romance, the onset of pain, the breakup of a family, the desolation of bereavement, picking up some sinful habit—any of these provides an opening for the fox to make us doubt. These occurrences in life are common and tragic.

The black fox appears.

He comes with an attack on your faith. Where is God? What kind of God would allow this to happen to you? It's a bitter pill. There is Jesus in the upper room, visiting with his disciples at the Last Supper. To Simon, he says, Beware of the fox. "Simon, . . Satan has demanded to sift all of you like wheat, but I have prayed for you that your own faith may not fail" (Luke 22:31-32). Ah, there it is, the point of attack: Simon's faith. The fox will work on his faith in God.

Is God good? Would God allow this to happen if he were good? Does God care? Where is God now that you need him the most? The attack is upon faith in God and your own self-confidence. When your humanity is unveiled and you see your own weakness, you may speak disparagingly: "Look at me, look at my failure, look at my weakness—I'm no good to anyone. My strength is gone. I'm a failure." Then the fox tries to destroy your faith in humanity: "Everyone is a fraud. No one is real. What a terrible place is the world, and to think I have to live in this jungle!"

The fox comes next with an attack on your enthusiasm. Some quip that "a man is not normal unless he is a radical at the age of twenty-one and a conservative at the age of thirty-five."

We see youths, aflame with idealism. They could change the world, put color into the environment, strike the anvil like a hammer making their mark on their world. But then, as Leonard Griffith succinctly states, "Now look at us: we have become the anvil, the colorless environment. And such conformists we are, no longer individuals but a type whose personality, clothes, brains, and opinions are completely interchangeable with thousands of others of our type."[20]

Why should it be left up to the youth to dream, to dare, to take the leap of faith? The rest of us have lived longer and have seen the power of God at work in the world and in our lives and the lives of others. Yet, instead of becoming daring pilgrims of faith, we become spiritually timid and lose our zest for real faith experiences. This is the work of the black fox.

The fox comes with that wretched feeling of meaninglessness and doubt. Where is the abundant life promised by Jesus (John 10:10)? What's so abundant about wars and rumors of wars, racial hatred, murder, adultery, broken families, dope addiction, and blatant materialism? What's so abundant about losing your business or house or health or family? Write me a song and entitle it *Stop the World, I Want to Get Off* (title of a Broadway musical).

The black fox is with Simon, sinking beneath the waves of Galilee and saying "What's so great about this? I was coming to you, Lord, and now this!" (see Matt. 14:28-31). As onlookers we want to say: "But, Simon, the winds and waves were there all the time. All around you was the blackness of night which you now curse. The difference is not in your circumstances; it is in you, your point of focus, your point of concentration. Mull over your problems, and you'll sink every time. Concentrate on your strength with Christ, and you'll overcome the world."

Biblical visions of God have him "wrapped in light," accompanied by flashing fire (Ps. 104:2; Exod. 19; Ezek. 1). But surrounding that brilliant light is a cloud of darkness, to protect the people. At Mount Sinai, the people witnessed the lightning signifying God's presence, but they "stood at a distance, while Moses drew near to the thick darkness where God was" (Exod. 19:18-21). The people were afar off; God was veiled in darkness. Isn't that just like God? He reveals only as much as we can handle, lest we be burned up in the "consuming fire" (Heb. 12:29).

At midnight, Jacob was down in the wild black gorge of the Jabbok, wrestling with an ominous shadow. It was a terrible night. But when the morning came, he had discovered God (Gen. 32:22-32).

The captives from Judah plaintively cried,

> By the rivers of Babylon—
> there we sat down and there we wept
> when we remembered Zion.
> On the willows there
> we hung up our harps.
>
> *—Psalm 137:1-2*

Gone were the glory days of the exodus and the conquest. Behind them were the regal days of splendor under David and Solomon. "Where now is your God?" asked the Babylonian imperialists (cf. Ps. 42:3, 10; Isa. 36:18-20). One man knew. Jeremiah found God behind in the thick darkness. God was present and active in the destiny of Israel. Already God was making plans, not only for Israel's physical deliverance, but for a greater day, the day of the Lord and the coming of the Messiah (Jer. 29-30).

On another day, another cloud swallowed the earth in its awful blackness. Men crouched in fear while women cried. The earth quaked beneath helpless feet, and a man died between two thieves. But God was in that darkness.

The black fox is no match for the King who spoke from the abyss of nothingness in the dawning days of creation and said: "Let there be light" (Gen. 1:3). The black fox is no match for the "God who raises the dead" (2 Cor. 1:9).

Writing about the Lord Jesus Christ, John said: "In him was life, and the life was the light of all people. The light shines in the darkness, and the darkness did not overcome it" (John 1:4-5).

Indeed, it never will! So why let the black fox of doubt take the joy out of living? Why let that fox use us to keep others out of the kingdom when they see us wallowing in our defeats?

Let me but live my life from year to year,
With forward face and unreluctant soul,
Nor hastening to, nor turning from the goal;
Nor mourning things that disappear.
In the dim past, nor holding back in fear.
From what the future veils; but with a whole
And happy heart, that pays its toil
To youth and age, and travels on with cheer.[21]

The King can make us cheerful if we will surrender our lives, our circumstances, our hopes, our dreams, and our fears to him who said,

All authority in heaven and on earth
has been given to me. . . .
And remember, I am with you always,
to the end of the age.

—*Matthew 28:18, 20*

FOR REFLECTION

The Black Fox of Doubt

Doubt can be debilitating. It is not unusual for a Christian to experience doubt. When we hear critics attack God's Word, we may wonder, "Is the Bible really true?" In confusion over unanswered prayer, we may ask, "Is God real? Does God really answer prayer?" When confronted with the reality of our own sinful desires, we may have doubts: "Has God really saved me?"

In spite of the tendency to doubt, we can be encouraged because honest doubt often leads to solid faith and deeper commitment.

Satan can use doubt as a destructive tool. He caused doubt in the garden of Eden by asking, "Did God say?" (Gen. 3:1). Satan will afflict us with doubts where and when we are the most vulnerable. Spiritual disobedience, disappointment, depression, illness, and even the fear of old age can trigger doubt.

The opposite of doubt, is faith. James encouraged those who were passing through trials to "ask God" and "ask in faith" (James 1:5-6).

ENCOURAGEMENT FROM SCRIPTURE

If any of you is lacking in wisdom, ask God, who gives to all generously and ungrudgingly, and it will be given you. But ask in faith, never doubting, for the one who doubts is like a wave of the sea driven and tossed by the wind; for the doubter, being double-minded and unstable in every way, must not expect to receive anything from the Lord.

—James 1:5-8

Jesus said to him, "Have you believed because you have seen me? Blessed are those who have not seen, and yet have come to believe."

—John 20:29

*And without faith it is impossible to please God,
for whoever would approach him must believe that
he exists and that he rewards those who seek him.*
                                                    —Hebrews 11:6

Fools say in their hearts, "There is no God."
                                                    —Psalm 14:1

*But now thus says the Lord, he who created you, O Jacob,
he who formed you, O Israel: Do not fear, for I have re-
deemed you; I have called you by name, you are mine.
When you pass through the waters, I will be with you;
and through the rivers, they shall not overwhelm you;
when you walk through fire you shall not be burned,
and the flame shall not consume you. For I am the Lord
your God, the Holy One of Israel, your Savior. I give
Egypt as your ransom, Ethiopia and Seba in exchange
for you.*
                                                    —Isaiah 43:1-3

Notes

1. George Burrowes, *The Song of Solomon* (Carlisle, Pa.: The Banner of Truth, 1973 reprint of the 1853 original), 310-312, quoted, adapted, and supplemented.

2. Alfred Lord Tennyson, "Vivien," in *The Complete Poetical Works* (Chicago: The Dominion Co., 1897), 632.

3. Albert E. Elliott, "Help Me Forget," in *Poems of Comfort* (Toronto: McClelland & Stewart Limited, 1948), 20.

4. Charles R. Swindoll, *Growing Strong in the Seasons of Life* (Portland, Ore.: Multnomah, 1983), 21.

5. Swindoll, 22.

6. Kathleen Mahoney, *Simple Wisdom* (New York: Viking Studio Books, 1993), 66.

7. Ruth Harms Calkin, *Love Is So Much More, Lord* (Elgin, Ill.: David C. Cook, 1979), 144.

8. Milton Layden, *Escaping the Hostility Trap* (Englewood Cliffs, N.J.: Prentice Hall, 1977), 2.

9. James M. Boice, *God the Redeemer* (Downers Grove, Ill.: InterVarsity Press, 1978), 95.

10. C. Roy Angell, *The Price Tags of Life* (Nashville: Broadman, 1959), 25-26.

11. Billy Graham, *The Billy Graham Christian Worker's Handbook* (Minneapolis, Minn.: World Wide Publications, 1984), 31.

12. Corrie ten Boom, in *The Great Compromise*, by Greg Laurie (Dallas: Word Publishing, 1994), 171.

13. Charles R. Swindoll, *Come Before Winter and Share My Hope* (Portland, Ore.: Multnomah, 1985), 188.

14. John Gillespie Magee Jr., "High Flight," *in Wings of Joy*, ed.

Joan Winmill Brown (Old Tappan, N.J.: Fleming H. Revell, 1977), 149.

15. Theodore (Teddy) Roosevelt, "Failures," in Swindoll, *Growing Strong*, 250-251.

16. Paul Tournier, *Learn to Grow Old* (New York: Harper & Row, 1972), 147.

17. William Dyal, *It's Worth Your Life* (New York: Association Press, 1967), 72.

18. Anna Eleanor Roosevelt, *You Learn by Living* (New York: Harper & Brothers, 1960), 29-30.

19. Graham, 100.

20. Leonard Griffith, *God in Man's Experience* (Waco: Word Books, 1968), 181.

21. Henry Van Dyke, in *The Radiant Road: Selections in Prose and Verse* (London: Bagster House, 1930), 69.

Author

W. Barry Miller has earned a doctorate in education from the University of Florida and has proven himself as a distinguished educator, author, newspaper columnist, and public speaker. He has served as a public school teacher, a curriculum and research specialist, and a superintendent of schools.

Miller serves internationally as an educational consultant and has been acclaimed for his educational leadership.

Barry and his wife, Loris, and their family are members of the Hanwell Baptist Church in Fredericton, New Brunswick, Canada. Barry is appreciated as an effective church leader and is licensed as a church minister.